RUMER GODDEN AND BLAC[K]

RUMER GODDEN: INTRODU[CTION]

EUROPEANS SETTLE DOWN IN DARJEELING 8

ZINGLAM OF RUMER GODDEN 25

RUMER GODDEN, THE WRITER 29

TEA-PLANTERS OF DARJEELING 35

GREENSHIELD BECOMES A NUNNERY 38

CONCLUSION 40

EPILOGUE: DARJEELING TODAY 42

Rumer Godden and Black Narcissus

(Revised and Enlarged Edition)

by

Colonel G.L. Rai-Zimmdar

Copyright 2012 by G.L. Rai-Zimmdar

All Rights Reserved

No part of this book may be used or reproduced, stored in a retrieval system, or transmitted in any form by any means, electronic, mechanical, photocopy, recording or otherwise, without written permission except in the case of brief quotation embodied in critical articles or reviews.

Dedicated

to

The Kirati Mongolians of Nepal

But history is also the narratives of grace, the recountings of those blessed and inexplicable moments when someone did something for someone else, saved a life, gave something beyond what was required by circumstance.

Thomas Cahill

Rumer Godden: Introduction

Dame Rumer Godden's first published work was aptly titled "Rungli-Rungliot" wherein she had sketched autobiographical accounts of her early days in a tea estate in Darjeeling. It projects with greater emphasis her own state of mind, still unsettled and perhaps somewhat bitter at the state of her affairs. However, Rungli-Rungliot has simply vanished from circulation but reappeared more than a decade later in a redacted and more humane reincarnation entitled "This Far and Not Farther".

Somewhat naively Rumer Godden explains that the new title is the literal translation of the former, but with the license of a fiction writer. Rungli-Rungliot is actually a Lepcha phrase, "Rhee-nung-li-yat" (anglicised by the British administrators as Rungli-Rungliot), which actually means "Returned from here". In other words, "here" indicates the easternmost frontiers of Nepal from where the Gurkhas had withdrawn after the Treaty of Sagauli was signed.

Black Narcissus, Rumer Godden's third book based on Rungli-Rungliot was written by her to celebrate her father's love life. The principal character of the novel Kanchhi was actually, in all fairness to her, her own step-mother, although Rumer Godden has pointedly referred to Kanchhi as only a concubine. Be that as it may, it is beyond any speculation that Kanchhi was indeed the Black Narcissus and the theme of the novel.

Rungli-Rungliot has the most attractive east-facing facade found ideally suited for a botanical garden. The Brits had "secured" permission from the Maharaja of Sikkim to establish a sanatorium in Darjeeling for the convalescing British soldiers. The climate of Darjeeling was found entirely salubrious enough by the Brits to declare it the summer capital of the province of Bengal. In addition, they also established Lloyd Botanical Garden in Rungli-Rungliot, named after Lieutenant Lloyd of the Royal Engineers, the Founder of the City of Darjeeling.

To this Botanical Garden of Rungli-Rungliot had arrived Miss Marianne North and painted an endemic flower which can be seen on display today at Royal Botanic Garden at Kew. Miss North had traveled round the world between

1871 and 1884 painting local flora and had donated her entire collection of 848 oil paintings to Kew Gardens.

Lloyd's Botanical Garden of Rungli-Rungliot was later moved to its present location in Darjeeling for administrative convenience and the land vacated by the Botanical Garden was immediately reappropriated as Rungli-Rungliot tea estate.

Brian Houghton Hodgson (1800-94) was posted as Post Master and Assistant to The Resident in Kathmandu while still a teenager. He was a self-taught man with only four years of formal education upon which he had added one year of training at East India Company College at Herefordshire before setting sails to India.

Hodgson was a remarkable man with ascetic devotion to everything cerebral and to him goes the singular credit of discovering the hitherto unknown original literature pertaining to Mahayana Buddhism.

It was Hodgson who believed in the suitability of colonizing the Eastern Himalayas and upon his recommendations many Europeans settled down to farm lands in the District of Darjeeling; Rumer Godden's father was one of them. Now read on...

Europeans settle down in Darjeeling

Recommendations of Brian H. Hodgson Esq., Her Majesty's Resident, Kathmandu, Nepal, Colonization of the Eastern Himalaya (or the District of Darjeeling) by Europeans, 1856[1].

.

As the interesting subject of the fitness of the Himalaya for European colonization is beginning to excite attention of the individuals and of the Government, it may be worth while to state distinctly my own conviction on the subject, together with the chief grounds of the conviction, because I have resided some thirty years in the Central and Eastern parts of the range, and have also served awhile in the Western, and all that time my attention has been directed to studies calculated to make my observation and experience more effective.

I say, then, unhesitatingly, that the Himalaya generally is very well calculated for the settlement of Europeans, and I feel more and

[1] Brian H. Hodgson: Essays on The Languages, Literature and Religion of Nepal and Tibet; Published 1874, Page 83.

more convinced that the encouragement of colonization therein is one of the highest and most important duties of the Government.

In the long, and throughout the globe quite unparalleled, gradation and heights, from the plains to the snows, every variety of climate is found with correspondent capabilities for the successful culture of various products suited to the wants of Europeans, for their own consumption or for profitable sale; and in this extraordinary gradation of heights, the high and the low are juxtaposed in a manner alike favourable to the labours of the healthful and to the relief of the ailing.

A healthy cultivator of our race could have his dwelling at four to six thousand feet, and his farms, both there and at various higher and lower elevations, yet still close to his abode; so that quasi-tropical and quasi-European products might be raised by him with the greatest facility; and in defect of health and strength, the colonist, like the visitor, would enjoy the vast advantage of entirely changing his climate without cost or fatigue of journey, besides having the additional resource of easy access to medicinal waters of universal diffusion and of proved efficacy in many kinds of ailments. The greatest variety of climate has of course relation to the transverse section of the Himalaya, or that from plains to snows; but the longitudinal section, or the S.E. and N.W. one, likewise presents as much and the same variety of climate as is proper to the plains in Bengal, Benares, and the north-western provinces; and it is quite a mistake to allege of the South-East Himalayas, or of Bengal, that their climate differs only for the worse from the drier climate at the hills or plains further west and north.

Undoubtedly, the South-East Himalaya has much less sun and much more moisture than the North-West Himalaya. But those Europeans, who have experienced the effects of climate of both, frequently prefer that of the former, and it is quite certain that, in the past twenty years, the South-East Himalaya has suffered much less epidemics, and has also enjoyed a complete exemption from those severe dysentries and fevers which have afflicted the denizens of the North-West Himalaya. It is as certain that the obscured sun of the South-East Himalaya is the cause of the difference, and that, though our clouds and mists may hurt our popular reputation with strangers, they are welcome to ourselves from their experienced and admitted beneficialness. Cloudy and misty as is our climate for five to six months, rheumatism and pulmonary affections are unknown. That the Himalaya, generally speaking is a region eminently healthful, can be doubted by no competent judge, and is demonstrable at once, and readily, by pointing to the finely developed muscles, pure skins, cheerful countenances, and universally well-formed strong-boned bodies of the native inhabitants, whose health and strength, and capacity of enduring toil and carrying heavy burdens, are as notorious, as are their exemption from bodily malformations and from most of the direst diseases to which flesh is heir, as well in the tropics as in the high latitudes of Europe --- results owing to the preeminent equability and temperateness of the climates, added to the simple active habits of the people.

The fearful epidemics of the plains seldom penetrate the Himalayas, which, moreover, seem to have a positive exemption from endemic diseases, or those proper to any given country. For forty years cholera has ravaged the plains continually almost. But in all that period Nepal has been visited only twice and Darjeeling scarcely at all. In the same forty years in Kathmandu, only two deaths (Mr.Stuart and Lieut Young) have occurred among Europeans, and both those were occasioned by diseases wholly apart from local influences; and in the escort of the Resident, the salubrity in my time was so great, that promotion came hardly to be calculated on at all, and a Sepahee would be Sepahee still, after fifteen to twenty years' service.

The Civil medical statistics of Nepal, as of Darjeeling, have always told the same story; if the Military statistics of the latter place have been, till lately, less favourable, the reason of this had nothing to do with the hill climate, but resulted wholly from the senseless selection of cases sent up; the absurd neglect of seasons in sending up and taking down of the invalids; and lastly, the shameful abandonment of all care and supervision of the men on the way up and down.

The appearance of European children at Darjeeling might alone suffice to prove the suitableness of the climate of the Himalaya at six to eight thousand feet for European colonization, confirmed, as such evidence is, by that of the aspect and health of such adult Europeans as came here with uninjured constitutions, and have led an active life since their arrival. Finer specimen of manly vigour the world could not show; and though none of the individuals I allude to have lately toiled all day in the open air at agricultural labours, yet I am credibly informed that some of them did for several years after their arrival here, and with perfect impunity; their agricultural pursuits having been abandoned for reasons quite apart from either injured health or inability to support themselves and families comfortably by such labours.

That Europeans would sustain injury from exposure during agricultural labours at any period of the year, seems therefore refuted by fact; and when it is remembered that such persons would be working here, as at home, amid an indigenous arboreal vegetation of oaks, hollies, chestnuts, sycamores, elms, horn-beams, birches, alders, elders, willows, and, more westerly, pines and firs, such a fact derives from such an analogy double strength; and the attempted inference from both is further justified by the healthful growth in the Himalaya of such of our own cereals and vegetables and fruits as we have thus far tried to introduce, with the sole exception of delicate and soft pulped fruits, not of an early or spring maturing kind, such as peaches, grapes, and the like. These rot, instead of ripening in the central region of the Himalaya, owing to the tropical rains and rarity of sun-shine at the ripening season.

But such soft fruits as become mature before the rains set in, as strawberries, come to perfection, as do all hard fruits, such as apples. There is, in fact, no end of the mineral and vegetable wealth of the Himalaya, and if the absence of flat ground, with the severity of the tropical monsoon or rainy season, present considerable drawback to agricultural success, on the other hand the endless inequality of surface offer a variety of temperature and of exposure, together with signal modification even of the element of moisture and rain, all highly conducive to the advantageous cultivation of numerous and diverse products proper to the soil or imported from elsewhere.

Temperature changes regularly in the ratio of 3 degree diminution of heat every thousand feet of height gained; and every large ridge crossing the course of the monsoon modifies almost as remarkably the amount of rain in the several tracts covered by such ridges. The ratio of decrease of heat with elevation, which has just been stated, must however be remembered to be an average and to have reference to the shade, not to the sun, for it has been found that the direct rays of the sun are as powerful at Darjeeling as in the plains, owing probably to the clearness of our atmosphere; and this is the reason why our clouds are so welcome and beneficial during the hottest months of the year. In other words, the constant cloudiness of that season is beneficial to the European. It is otherwise, however, as regards his crops, which being ripening at that period, would be benefited by a clearer sky; and thus it is that a certain degree of oppugnancy exists between the sites most congenial to the European and to his crops; for, whilst at height of six to seven thousand, perhaps, might be most congenial to him, one of four to five thousand would certainly suit them better, not so much for the average higher temperature, as for the larger supply of sun-shine. But the oppugnancy is only one of degree, and whilst four thousand is a very endurable climate for the European, there is no reason why he should not have his abode, as is the frequent custom of the country, at a somewhat higher level than that of his fields, should he find such an arrangement advantageous upon the whole.

The fertility of the soil is demonstrated by the luxuriance of the arboreal and shrub vegetation, a luxuriance as great in degree as universal in prevalence. True this luxuriance has its evils and, in its present unpruned state, may be one great cause why the feeding of flocks and herds is scantily pursued by the people, and without much success, speaking generally; for there are exceptions even now, and European energy would soon multiply these exceptions, besides grappling successfully with the presumed source of the evil, or too much and too rank vegetation, not to add, that, in the district next the snows and Tibet, that hyper-luxuriance ceases, and herds and flocks abound, and the latter yield fleeces admirable for their fineness or length of fibre. The soil consists of a deep bed of very rich vegetable mould from one to three feet deep, to preserve which from being carried away by the tropical rains after the removal of its natural cover of forest and under-growth, by terracing and other known expedients, must be the colonist's first care, for the underlying earth is almost always a hungry red clay but happily one whose tenacity and poverty are much qualified by better ingredients derived from the debris of the gneisses and schists that constitute the almost sole rocks. The argillaceous constituents of the soil are perhaps in good proportion; the siliceous, perhaps, rather too abundant; the calcereous deficient. Heretofore, the superficial mould has been the sole stay of the agriculturist and floriculturist. How far that would continue to be the case under abler culture, I know not. But, so long as it did continue, the caution above given would demand the most vigilant and incessant attention.

The common European cereals, or wheat, barley, rye, and oats, are little heeded in the Himalaya, where I never saw crops equal those grown in various parts of the plains. But this, though no doubt attributable in some measure to a deal of the Himalayan population being located at heights above those where, in the present forest encumbered state of the country, a sufficiency of summer sun for such crops can be safely calculated upon, is likewise attributable in part to the preference for rices, maizes, sorghums, panicums or millet, buck-wheat, and amaranth, on the part of the people, whose cultivation of wheat is most careless, without manure, even in double-cropped and old lands, and the plant is allowed to be over-run, whilst growing, by wild hemp or artemesia, or other social weed of most frequent occurrence in the Himalaya. Observe too, that the system of double cropping now occasions the sacrifice of the despised wheat crop which is a spring one to the cherished autumnal crop which is a rice one; and that were the former allowed due consideration and treated with reference to its furnishing a main article of food, instead of being regarded merely with reference to the still, as is now very generally the case among the native population, we might reasonably expect to see fine crops of wheat as high at least as five thousand feet and more, especially so when the clearance of the land, conducted judiciously, was enabled to produce its due and experienced effects in augmenting the sun-shine and diminishing the rain and mist in such properly cleared tracts. Heretofore, skill and energy have done absolutely nothing, in these or other respects, for Himalayan agriculture, and yet there is no country on earth where more advantage might be derived from skill and energy applied to the culture of agricultural products. As already said, the infinite variety of elevation and of exposure (both as to heat and moisture), together with the indefinite richness of the soil, as proved by indigenous tree and shrub and other vegetation, are premises one can hardly fail to rest soundly upon in prognosticating the high success of European culture of the Himalayan slopes, notwithstanding the drawbacks I have enumerated. There need hardly be any end to the variety of products, and good success must attend the cultivation of many of them, after a little experience shall have taught the specialties of the soil and climate, so that the subject should be incessantly agitated till the Government and the public are made fully aware of the merits. How much iteration is needed, may be illustrated by the simple mention of the fact, that the fitness of the Himalayas for tea-growing was fully ascertained twentyfive years ago in the valley of Nepal, a normal characteristic region, as well in regard to position as to elevation. Tea seeds and plants were procured from China through the medium of the Cashmere merchants then located in Kathmandu. They were sown and planted in the Residency garden, where they flourished greatly, flowering and seeding as usual, and moreover, grafts ad libitum were multiplied by means of the nearly allied Eurya (Camelia) kisi, which in the valley of Nepal, as elsewhere, throughout the Himalaya, is an indigenous and most abundant species. These favourable results were duly announced at the time of Dr. Abel, Physician to the Governor General, an accomplished person, with special qualification. And yet, in spite of all this, twenty years were suffered to elapse before any effective notice of so important an experiment could be obtained.

I trust, therefore, that the general subject of the high capabilities of the climate and soil of the Himalayas, and their eminent fitness for European colonization having once been taken up, will never be dropped till colonization is a "fait accompli" and that the accomplishment of this greatest, surest, soundest, and simplest of all political measures for the stabilisation of the

British power in India, may adorn the annals of the present Viceroy's administration.

But observe, I do not mean wholesale and instantaneous colonization, for any such I regard as simply impossible; nor, were it possible, would I advocate it. The distance and unpopularity of India, however, would preclude all rational anticipation of any such colonization, whatever might be the wish to effect it. What I mean is, looking to these very obstacles and drawbacks, seeming and real, that some systematic means should be used to reduce their apparent and real dimentions, to make familiarly and generally known the cheapest methods and actual cost of reaching India; to afford discriminating aid in some cases towards reaching it and settling in it; and to shew that, in regard to the Himalaya, the vulgar dread of Indian diseases is wholly baseless --- to show also, that its infinite variety of juxtaposed elevations, with correspondent differences of climate, both as to heat and moisture, and the unbounded richness of its soil at all elevations, offer peculiar and most unique advantages (not a fiftieth part of the surface being now occupied) to the colonists, as well on the score of health as on that of opportunity, to cultivate a wonderful variety of products ranging from the tropical nearly to the European.

A word as to the native population, in relation to the measure under contemplation. In the first place, the vast extent of unoccupied land would free the Government from the necessity of providing against wrongful displacement; and, in the second place, the erect spirit and freedom from disqualifying prejudices, proper to the Himalayan population, would at once make their protection from European oppression easy, and would render them readily subservient under the direction of European energy and skill to the more effectual drawing forth of the natural resources pf the region. Located himself at an elevation he might find most conducive to his health, the colonist might, on the very verge of the lower region, effectually command the great resources for traffic in timber, drugs, dyes, hides, horns, ghee, and textile materials, not excluding silk, which that region affords; whilst, if he chose to locate himself further from the plains and devote himself to agriculture and sheep-breeding, he might make his election among endless sites in the central and higher region of the Himalaya, of a place where these or those sorts of cereal flourished best, and where cattle and sheep could be reared, under circumstances of surface, vegetation, and temperature as various as the imagination can depict, but all more or less propitious; the steep slopes and abundant vegetation, rank but nutritious, of the central region, giving place, in the higher region, to a drier air, a more level surface, and a scanter and highly aromatic vegetation, peculiarly suited to sheep and goats, whose fleeces in the region would well repay the cost of transport to the most distant markets.

Not that I would in general hold out to the colonists the prospect of growing rich by the utmost use of the above indicated resources for the accumulation of wealth --- to which might, and certainly in due course would, be added those of the Trans-Himalayan commerce --- but would rather fix his attention, primarily, at least upon the certain prospect of comfort, of a full belly, a warm back, and a decent domicile, or, in other words, of food, clothes, and shelter for himself, his wife, and children, unfailing with the most ordinary prudence and toil, and such, as to quality and quantity, as would be a perfect god- send to the starving peasantry of Ireland and of the Scotch Highlanders. These are the settlers I would, but without discouraging the others, primarily encouraged by free grants for the first five years, and by a light rent upon long and fixed leases thereafter, looking to compensation in the general prestige of their known forthcomingness on the spot, and assured that, with the actual backing upon occasions of political stress and difficulty of some fifty to one hundred thousand loyal hearts and stalwart bodies of Saxon mould, our empire in India might safely defy the world in arms against it.

(Quoted with permission).

Zinglam of Rumer Godden

Brian Hodgson's report was received and welcomed with enthusiasm, it attracted serious candidates and soon enough every hills and valleys of the District of Darjeeling were filled with Europeans farmers. They came well prepared equipped with new technologies and farming methods in dairy farming to animal husbandry and poultry farming; they brought their own breed of cows, pigs and poultry birds. They installed methane gas plants using cow-dung, dammed small rivulets and began to generate electricity for domestic use.

While all these were looking very encouraging, they soon discovered they could not compete with the local Nepalese farmers in per capita income; the locals were frugal and they 'knew' what to plant and when to harvest.

Just as this competition was going full speed, the Brits had smuggled out tea seed from China and were experimenting with tea plants. Dr Campbell had experimented with the seeds from China and found them growing extremely well in his backyard in Kathmandu. The Brits had even smuggled out some Chinese Tea Planters and were able to establish Demonstration Farms and learn from them how to plant and harvest tea.

About the same time, Major Bruce and Mr Scott independently discovered there were tea bushes growing wild in Assam, north-eastern corner of India.

The European farmers were quick to take the best advantage of time and giving up competing with the local farmers turned to tea farming. It demanded higher input in terms of capital goods which the Nepalese farmers could not afford and from then on tea industry in India became the Brits monopoly and that is where we meet Mr Godden, the tea-planter.

Messrs Kilburn & Co owned a group of three tea estates; and while Namring is the seat of the Manager and where the tea is actually manufactured, Poomong and Zinglam are leaf gardens managed by Assistant Managers. Zinglam however, has the singular distinction of carrying two proper names: it is also popularly known as Zimlang and either of the two names is officially accepted.

Rumer Godden had lived in Zinglam long enough and is sure to have witnessed the farmers festival the local Gurkhas hold once every year on the Winter Solstice day at the confluence of River Teesta and Rangeet. This celebration is the memorial to the "Washing of

Kukri" in 1792 by the Gurkhas to ceremonially declare the end of bloodshed and demarking River Teesta as the boundary between Nepal and Bhutan.

Rungli-Rungliot is situated on the lower spur that leads directly eastward and away from Tiger Hill, a touristy place now. The Gurkhas had established their Observation Post on Tiger Hill from where the most remarkable sunrise in the world could be viewed at three in the morning; the sun is seen rising when it is still beyond the International Date Line. Rumer Godden used to go on picnic to a place called "Durpin Danra" on the same ridge running down from Tiger Hill, where the ridge abruptly ends in a magnificent precipice; Durpin Danra was the Gurkhas' last outpost. On a clear day, one can see from Durpin Danra, across the small stretch of Indian soil at its feet, the plains of Bangla Desh and far into South China Sea and beyond.

Rungli-Rungliot is an extensive tea growing sub-division within the District of Darjeeling and Zinglam is one of the six tea estates within the sub-division. Rumer Godden did not pick up Zinglam at random, her story is revealed in the following chapters.

The concept of the tea gardens of Darjeeling was established on the premise that it will forever remain part of the Empire, as was visualized by Brian Hodgson; their demise therefore, was innate in its formation. The parent companies with their capital in pound sterling were based in the UK which implied their accounts would be audited under British domestic law; profits were therefore, calculated and disbursed in the UK. This system became untenable when India was granted Independence and the Tea Planters were obliged to leave; tea gardens were simply left to the highest bidders, of which there were not many.

This arrangement has left behind a lasting legacy; a faulty system of collection of taxes in India. While the Empire lasted, the Brits paid taxes direct to the Crown in England and Indian subjects were virtually left outside the gambit of taxation. The psychology of paying income tax, therefore has remained alien to the psyche of Indian citizens. Government servants are obliged to pay the income tax, it is deducted at source, only a small percentage of Indian citizens pay income tax today.

Rumer Godden, the Writer

Rumer Godden had donated her first book, "Rungli-Rungliot" to the Armed Forces which was published by Penguins in its paperback edition for free distribution among His Majesty's Armed Forces during World War II.

At the outset of the World War II, both the young Assistant Managers of Zinglam and Poomong had volunteered to join the Army and the Manager was obliged to fill the vacancy locally. Strange as it may sound now, the replacement Gurkha Assistant Managers were given the title of Munshi (reminescent of Queen Victoria's personal Munshi) and of course, much less remuneration. Rumer Godden mentions the son of this Munshi of Zinglam had received King's Commission but it is very unlikely they ever met.

Rumer Godden's father was the Manager of neighbouring Tea Estate called Gielle, owned by Messrs Davenport & Co before he went down to the Plains to manage a jute mill.

In those halcyon days, the Managers were virtual Kings of their domains and most of them, the Managers of tea estates in Darjeeling were married to local Gurkha women. Rumer Godden's host, the Manager of Namring too was married to a Gurkha wife and although she met the Gurkha Mem on several occasions, Godden refuses to introduce the Mem in her books. They were not just 'kept women' for many Managers had taken great care to see their wives were comfortably absorbed into western culture and when they retired, many of these women accompanied their husbands into retirement in the UK. Godden did mention however, that the Manager of Namring, her host, enjoyed all the trappings of a Maharaja.

Mr Godden Sr too had taken a Gurkha woman to wife and she must have been a celebrated beauty as this ditty makes the claims:

Kirket ko muni, Saab le khelne tennis ko ramro game,

Jor kantha mathi tilhari laune Godden ko Kanchhi mem.

Roughly translated, the couplet means "Sa-abs play beautiful game of tennis with little less enthusiasm than they play cricket. It brings to mind the beautiful Kanchhi Mem of Godden bedecked with 'jor-kanthha and tilahari' (golden ornaments favoured by Gurkha women of Eastern Nepal.) The ditty can also be interpreted that perhaps, Mr Godden's Kanchhi Mem stole the show whether the Sa'abs were playing cricket or tennis.

Just above Rungli-Rungliot, along the road to Darjeeling, are to be seen even today, massive dressed rocks lined up as retainer wall. Actually, we would be traveling along the base of the Gurkha Fort, which the locals simply call Garhi, or fort. The Fort was abandoned by the Gurkhas when the Treaty of Peace and Friendship was signed and razed to the ground. Eventually, when peace finally prevailed, a cantonment for the British and the Gurkha soldiers was established on its lower flanks.

The rocks forming the retainer wall are igneous rocks whereas the entire Himalayan Range is made up of sedimentary rocks. This supports the old Kirati legend that the hill tops of Tiger Hills and Garhi were once active volcanoes. As the volcanoes became dormant, their mouths were sealed when the molten lava cooled down and lakes were formed in the cavity. These lakes have now become the primary source of drinking water for the citizens of the City of Darjeeling.

Recently, a local biologist Mr Bharat Rai has made a startling discovery; he has discovered presence of salamanders, now known as Bharat Rai's salamanders, in the marshy areas near the lakes of Tiger Hill. Once again, this discovery supports the popular folklore that salamanders actually live in volcanoes.

When the District of Darjeeling was under the Gurkhas, the most popular ownership of land was acquired through a system known to them as "khurpa-thyak", literally speaking "machete-mark", where a prospective land owner would claim ownership of a track of land holding simply by scraping tree bark with a machete and leaving a distinctive charcoal mark upon it; the District of Darjeeling used to be then a primary forest. Rumer Godden alters the equation and mentions that a certain Gurkha Prince, General Dilip Rai had acquired his tract of land from the British Government on lease.

The Gurkhas knew of the sunrise at three o'clock in the morning, Tiger Hill used to be their Observation Post. Of the sunrise from Tiger Hill Mark Twain wrote, "….a sight you may never wish to trade with any other scenery of the world."

This was the background of Kanchhi upon which Rumer Godden wrote her famously complicated romantic fiction "Black Narcissus"; Kanchhi was none other than, we might as well in all fairness say, her own step-mother. Rumer Godden had an eye to celebrate her father's love life in this book and her stay in Zinglam was evidently in an effort to research and authenticate the background.

Not only Kanchhi, but the entire dramatis personae of Black Narcissus, from General Dilip Rai to Colonel Pratap Rai and from Sannyasi and the grooms to the farmhands are Gurkhas. None but the Gurkhas would call the Nuns "Lamenis" which actually means "Female Lamas" in their language and Godden opted to use the Gurkha word Lamenis to describe the nuns.

Unfortunately, the film-wallahs have managed to totally ruin the integrity of her novel while they Indianised the entire background stage-settings to the extent that not even a slightest hint of their ethnic identity as Gurkhas remain. Rumer Godden was terribly disappointed at the film version of her book but she knew she could do nothing about it.

Although this is a strictly personal matter to the Goddens, a part of their family history, but it is perhaps better the movie has treated them anonymously in the realm of a fairytale. No Kanchhi will stand up to demand recognition for she had briefly sparkled like a dew drop on a leaf never to be seen again by another human eye.

Tea-Planters of Darjeeling

Following Brian Hodgson's recommendations, several Europeans arrived in Darjeeling around the eighteen-forties to stake out claims on the title of the land they would farm. Sooner they found they could not profitably compete with the local Gurkha farmers and turned to growing and manufacturing tea which demanded capital investment the Gurkhas could not afford. Soon, very soon, tea industry took over the district; besides proving Brian Hodgson right, Darjeeling became the focal point of all activities related to fine tea that till this date Darjeeling has remained synonymous to finest tea.

The tea-planters were an exclusive breed of go-getters, who represented the fine spirit of the Empire in its best. They loved sports for its own sake and they worked very hard and played very hard. Polo, the game of Princes as is known today was "invented" by the tea-planters as a brass plaque on the walls of a Gardener's Club at Silchar declare. Samson-Way, a young Assistant Manager holds world record unbeaten till this date, of catching a 121 lb golden mahseer on his rod and line.

World War II movie fans would happily recall the covert operation conducted by the tea-planters, many of them from the tea gardens of Darjeeling. The episode was depicted quite realistically in its movie version Sea-Wolves. During World War II, the covert group had blown up the German communication ship s.s.Ehrenfels anchored off the coast of neutral Goa. War Office had gathered enough evidence to believe that s.s.Ehrenfels was engaged in passing on maritime information to German U-boats who in turn hunted down and sank the Allied merchant ships. Of particular interest is the fate of the ship s.s.Gairsoppa, which was carrying a cargo of 80 tons of silver ingots from India to the UK when it was sunk by the U-boats on Feb 16, 1941 and none but s.s.Ehrenfels could have alerted the U-boats.

The Planters Club of Darjeeling is the watering hole for one and Europeans, thirsty or not. It used to be heard around the lounges of the Club that the Darjeeling Planters were hand picked for the Operation "Sea Wolves" for one vital qualification, that the Gurkha wives could be trusted to hold their peace during the month long absence of their spouse.

Greenshield as seen from the North-East, is surrounded by cryptomeria japonica trees many of them could have been planted by Miss Phyllis Hill and Miss Blanche Whitehall. Its ground floor was occupied by the students while its 'bobaji-khana' (kitchen and dining hall) are extended further on western side. There was a tennis court on its western ground and a fairly beautiful flower garden on eastern side.

One remarkable feature of this building is that one could watch the sunrise at three o'clock in the morning right from the bedroom windows.

Greenshield becomes a Nunnery

Two very resourceful English women, Miss Phyllis Hill and Miss Blanche Whitehall used to run a private boarding school called Greenshield, (its photograph appears on the cover of this booklet); it was located just above Rungli-Rungliot. Greenshield was exclusively run for the children of the Gurkha Mems and although Rumer Godden does not mention these two ladies of the Greenshield by name but has understandably transformed them into Irish Nuns running a convent which forms the epicentre of her novel Black Narcissus.

Without any feature in between to intervene, the vista of remarkably beautiful sunrise as seen from Tiger Hill and described above can also be viewed from the bedroom windows of Greenshield. It is not difficult to believe that Greenshield must have been so sited as with that prospect in mind.

In 1947 India was granted Independence and Miss Hill and Miss Whitehall had no option but to leave Greenshield, as all the rest of the Brits were leaving India for good. Apprehending an influx of non-citizens, Britain had prohibited its erstwhile colonial subjects from entering and settling down in UK. Very soon, it became clear that the tea-planters of Darjeeling too must leave and many a family was willy-nilly broken up. Eventually the children of the Gurkha Mems got absorbed into the main streams of life New India was offering while a handful of them have somehow managed to immigrate to their fatherland.

Greenshield itself immediately lost its identity as a Boarding School and nothing exists today except the building as a silent witness to the charmed life of the Gurkha Mems of the British tea-planters and their children.

Conclusion

To effectively seal off Nepal from the East and to maintain an active surveillance, the Brits had created the State of Sikkim carving it out from the older map of Greater Nepal. Sikkim, (originally Suk-Khim or "New Home" to the Gurkhas) had formed the easternmost province of Nepal with River Teesta as its boundary with Bhutan, (Bhotang to the Gurkhas). But, all these events had taken place a century before Rumer Godden's arrival at Zinglam.

Such were the time and life of Rumer Godden in Zinglam and even earlier in Gielle, the accounts of which she has conveniently excluded from all her literary works and that is the prerogative of a fiction writer which we ought to accept.

Black Narcissus is exclusively based on the one and only historical episode of the Brits ever inter-acting with the Gurkhas at social level. This fragment of the history of the Raj as Rumer Godden saw and lived through however, will very likely soon be forgotten and lost forever along with the memories of the wonderful days of the Empire in the remote tea gardens of Darjeeling.

Circumstances have been very unfavourable to the children of the Gurkha Mems, the alumni of Greenshield. The droplets of their memory have simply fallen into and got dissolved in the vast ocean of the story of the British Raj, lost forever.

Epilogue: Darjeeling Today

Nothing much has changed since Dame Rumer Godden walked the roads of Darjeeling; the same narrow roads, albeit dirtier and much more congested. Clusters of thatched roof huts form most of the villages as in her days, still without electricity and running water. Had it not been for the UNESCO, the picturesque Darjeeling Himalayan Railway would have been torn down; as it is its one half section connecting Siliguri with Gielle Khola has already been uprooted.

But this is the irony of fate; every acre of its land produces the world famous 'Champagne of Tea', the best tea in the world and together with the multitude of tourists that throng its streets, Darjeeling is the cash-cow amidst its not so fortunate neighbourly districts. Most of the famous tea produced in Darjeeling is sold discretely by the Government to its clients. Darjeeling once used to take pride as the Queen of the Hill Stations, has fallen from the grace in more than the last half a century quietly suffering the indignity of blinding neglect.

Neglect is not the only malignancy Darjeeling suffers from; Darjeeling which was envisioned by that maverick Brian Hodgson as a perfect piece of real estate recommended very suitable to be colonised by Europeans; eulogized by Mark Twain; the city where the famous actress Lady Vivien Leigh was born; but the malaise runs much deeper.

Soon after Independence, the Founding Fathers of Independent India had embarked upon very many ambitious projects for the upliftment of the country and its masses; one of them was to reorganize the country on the basis of language. Known as State Re-organization Commission of 1953, it mandated the map of India was to be redrawn on the basis of language. But, as the forte of the politicians of Calcutta, they fudged the census report and claimed Darjeeling as a contiguous part of West Bengal. Although, 99% of the citizens of Darjeeling are Nepali speaking ethnic Mongolians, the Calcutta politicians have successfully managed to hogwash the statistics and claim they are Bengalis.

Unfortunately, Federal Government of India has its own axe to grind and has chosen to turn a blind eye which allows the crafty politicians of Calcutta to continue to deny citizens of Darjeeling the justice Indian Constitution grants.

There is darkness, as goes the proverb, right under the lamp, as this is the account of how Human Rights is being violated with impunity at the very back yard of the land that gave birth to Gandhian Philosophy.